MODERN
CENTRAL
BANKING

SIMPLIFIED

Michael J. Panzner

This publication is designed to provide accurate and authoritative information in regard to the subject matter covered. It is sold with the understanding that neither the author nor the publisher is engaged in rendering legal, accounting, or other professional service. If legal advice or other expert assistance is required, the services of a competent professional should be sought. The opinions expressed are those of the author and do not necessarily reflect the views of any other individual or organization.

Copyright © 2012 by Michael J. Panzner

ISBN: 1469920506
ISBN-13: 978-1469920504

Cover photograph: Federal Reserve Bank
Cover design: Michael J. Panzner, in black & white, with lots of red ink all over

Print money.

Print money.

Print money.

Print money.

Print money.

Print money.

Print money.

Print money.

Print money.

Print money.

Print money.

Print money.

Print money.

Print money.

Print money.

Print money.

Print money.

Print money.

Print money.

Print money.

Print money.

Print money.

Print money.

Print money.

Print money.

Print money.

Print money.

Print money.

Print money.

Print money.

Print money.

Print money.

Print money.

Print money.

Print money.

Print money.

Print money.

Print money.

Print money.

Print money.

Print money.

Print money.

Print money.

Print money.

Print money.

Print money.

Print money.

Print money.

Print money.

Print money.

Print money.

Print money.

Print money.

Print money.

Print money.

Print money.

Print money.

Print money.

Print money.

Print money.

Print money.

Print money.

Print money.

Print money.

Print money.

Print money.

Print money.

Print money.

Print money.

Print money.

Print money.

Print money.

Print money.

Print money.

Print money.

Print money.

Print money.

Print money.

Print money.

Print money.

Print money.

Print money.

Print money.

Print money.

Print money.

Print money.

Print money.

Print money.

Print money.

Print money.

Print money.

Print money.

Print money.

Print money.

Print money.

Print money.

Print money.

Print money.

Print money.

Print money.

Print money.

Print money.

Print money.

Print money.

Print money.

Print money.

Print money.

Print money.

Print money.

Print money.

Print money.

Print money.

Print money.

Print money.

Print money.

Print money.

Print money.

Print money.

Print money.

Print money.

Print money.

Print money.

Print money.

Print money.

Print money.

Print money.

Print money.

Print money.

Print money.

Print money.

Print money.

Print money.

Print money.

Print money.

Print money.

Print money.

Print money.

Print money.

Print money.

Print money.

Print money.

Print money.

Print money.

Print money.

Print money.

Print money.

Print money.

Print money.

Print money.

Print money.

Print money.

Print money.

Print money.

Print money.

Print money.

Print money.

Print money.

Print money.

Print money.

Print money.

Print money.

Print money.

Print money.

Print money.

Print money.

Print money.

Print money.

Print money.

Print money.

Print money.

Print money.

Print money.

Print money.

Print money.

Print money.

Print money.

Print money.

Print money.

Print money.

Print money.

Print money.

Print money.

Print money.

Print money.

Print money.

Print money.

Print money.

Print money.

Print money.

Print money.

Print money.

Print money.

Print money.

Print money.

Print money.

Print money.

Keep on printing.

Made in the USA
Middletown, DE
19 November 2020